Elizabeth Stuart Phelps

The Supply at Saint Agatha's

Elizabeth Stuart Phelps

The Supply at Saint Agatha's

ISBN/EAN: 9783743350427

Manufactured in Europe, USA, Canada, Australia, Japa

Cover: Foto ©ninafisch / pixelio.de

Manufactured and distributed by brebook publishing software
(www.brebook.com)

Elizabeth Stuart Phelps

The Supply at Saint Agatha's

THE

SUPPLY AT SAINT AGATHA'S

BY

ELIZABETH STUART PHELPS

WITH ILLUSTRATIONS

BY

E. BOYD SMITH AND MARCIA OAKES WOODBURY

BOSTON AND NEW YORK
HOUGHTON, MIFFLIN AND COMPANY
The Riverside Press, Cambridge
1897

The Riverside Press, Cambridge, Mass., U. S. A.
Electrotyped and Printed by H. O. Houghton & Co.

THE SUPPLY AT SAINT AGATHA'S.

At the crossing of the old avenue with the stream of present traffic, in a city which, for obvious reasons, will not be identified by the writer of these pages, there stood — and still stands — the Church of Saint Agatha's.

The church is not without a history, chiefly such as fashion and sect combine to record. It is an eminent church, with a stately date upon its foundation stone, and a pew-list unsurpassed for certain qualities among the worshipers of the Eastern States. Saint Agatha's has long been distinguished for three things, its money, its music, and its soundness.

When the tax-list of the town is printed in the daily papers once a year, the wardens and the leading parishioners of Saint Agatha's stand far upwards in the score, and their names are traced by slow, grimy fingers of mechanics and strikers and socialists laboriously reading on Saturday nights.

The choir of Saint Agatha's, as all the world

knows, is superior. Her soprano alone (a famous prima donna) would fill the house. Women throng the aisles to hear the tenor, and musical critics, hat in hand, and pad on hat, drop in to report the anthem and the offertory for the Monday morning press.

In ecclesiastical position, it is needless to add, Saint Agatha's has always been above reproach. When did Saint Agatha's question a canon? When did she contend with a custom? When did she criticise a creed? Why should she contest a tradition? She accepts, she conforms, she prospers.

In one particular Saint Agatha's has been thrust into an attitude of originality foreign to her taste. Her leading men feel called upon occasionally to explain how the eternal feminine came — a little contrary to the fashion of our land — to be recognized in the name of the church. Saint Agatha's first pastor, one should know, was a very young man of enthusiastic and unconventional temperament. He did not live long enough to outgrow this — for a clergyman — unfortunate trend of nature, having died, full of dreams and visions, in the teeth of a lowering conflict with his wardens; but he lived long enough to carry the day and the name for a portion of his people who desired to call their church in honor of a sweet, though rich, old lady who had put her private fortune into their beautiful house of worship, and her warm heart into their future success. It had befallen this dear old lady to bear the name of Agatha, which, for her sake, — and, of course, in due ecclesiastical remembrance of the strictly canonical saint of similar cognomen, — was accordingly bestowed upon the church.

In the year of our Lord eighteen hundred and another numeral, which I am requested not to indicate, but I may not deny that it is a recent one, the popular rector of Saint Agatha's took a winter vacation. He was an imposing and imperious man, full of years and honors, in the full sway of his professional fame, when he fell a victim, like any common person, to the grippe.

In the attempt to recover from this vulgar malady, he was forced to observe that his select physician had drugged him, *via* an exclusive bronchitis, into a minister's sore throat, such as any ordinary country parson might develop for lack of an overcoat, or a fire in his bedroom. Without undue delay or reluctance, the rector of Saint Agatha's took ship for the south of France; and in the comfortable way in which such things are done in such quarters, the church was set trundling upon the wheels of a two-months' "supply." This was managed so gracefully by the experienced vestry of Saint Agatha's that hardly a visible jar occurred in the parish machinery. Many of the people did not know that their rector had gone until a canon from London sonorously filled the pulpit one Sunday morning. A distinguished Middle State clergyman followed the next week; the West sent her brightest and best the succeeding Sunday; and so it went.

Eminent variety easily occupied that sacred desk. The wardens of St. Agatha's have but to say, Come, and he cometh who weigheth the honor of ministering in this aristocratic pulpit. In brief, the most distinguished men in the denomination cordially supplied. On the whole, perhaps the parish enjoyed their rector's vacation as much as he did.

Now, upon the vestry there chanced at that time to be one man who was "different." One does find such people even among the officers of fashionable churches. This man (he was, by the way, a grand-nephew of the old lady who built the church when

Saint Agatha's was an unendowed experiment) had occasional views not wholly in harmony with the policy of his brother officers; and, being himself a heavy rate-payer, was allowed, sometimes, by the courtesy of the majority, — when his notion was not really in bad form, you know, — to have his way. He did not get it so often but that he was glad to make the most of it when he did; and when his turn came to control the supply for that Sunday with which this narrative has to do, he asked the privilege of being intrusted with the details of the business. This request, as from a useful man of certain eccentricities, was indulgently granted; and thus there occurred the events which I am privileged to relate.

It was just before Lent, and the winter had been a cold one. One Friday evening in early March there came up, or came down, a drifting snow-storm. It was bad enough in town, but in the suburbs it was worse, and in the country it was little less than dangerous to passengers through the wide, wind-swept streets, the choking lanes, and bitter moors.

An old clergyman, the pastor of a scattered parish, sat in his study on that Friday night, and

thanked God that the weekly evening service was
over, and his day's work done. He would have
regretted being called out again that night, for he
had got quite wet in walking to church and back,
and the cold from which he had been suffering for
a week past might not be benefited thereby. This
fact in itself was a matter of no concern, under ordinary conditions, to the old clergyman, who, being a
lonely man in a forlorn country boarding-house, with
nobody to take care of him, was accustomed to live
under the shadow of a " common cold," and who
paid no more attention to his own physical discom-
forts in the face of daily duty than he paid to the
latest fashion in sable trimmings in the front pews
at Saint Agatha's. There was no fur trimming on
his overcoat, which was seven years old and pitiably
thin. But he had been invited to supply at Saint
Agatha's next Sunday, and to that unexampled honor
and opportunity he gave the pathetic attention —
half personal pleasure, half religious fervor — of an
overlooked and devout man. In the course of a
forty-years' ministry he had not been asked to
preach in a city pulpit. The event was tremendous
to him. He had been agitated by the invitation,
which ran in some such way as this :

" He had been invited to supply at St. Agatha's."

. . . "In closing, permit me to say, sir, that it would be agreeable to us to welcome among us the grandson of our first pastor, that young rector who died in the bud of his youth and Christian originality. The fact of your ancestry will give to your presence a peculiar interest for our people at large. But I beg to be allowed to add on behalf of the committee, that certain qualities in yourself and in your own work have led us to believe that you may exert positive influences upon us of which we stand in need. In your remote and rural parish your life has not passed unobserved. Your labors as a pastor, and your methods of preaching, have been an object of study to some of us. We have come to rate you, sir, as one of the men of God. There are not many. In meeting with our people, the writer personally hopes that you may be able to teach us something of the secret of your own happy and successful experience as a minister of Christ our Lord." . . .

The old clergyman sat with his feet upon the base of his little cylinder coal-stove. His thin ankles shrank in the damp stockings which he had not been able to change since he came in out of the

storm, because, owing to some personal preference
of the laundress, he could not find any dry ones.
His worn slippers flapped upon his cold feet when
he moved. But he had on his flowered dressing-
gown of ancient pattern and rustic cut; his high
arm-chair was cushioned in chintz and excelsior
behind his aching head; the green paper shade was
on his study-lamp; his best-beloved books (for the
old saint was a student) lay within reach upon the
table; piled upon them were his manuscript sermons;
and he sighed with the content of a man who
feels himself to be, although unworthy, in the loving
arms of luxury.   A rap at the door undeceived him.
His landlady put in her withered face.

"Sir," she said, "the widder Peek's a-dying.
It's just like her to take a night like this — but
she's sent for you. I must say I don't call you fit
to go."

"A man is always fit to do his duty," said the
old clergyman, rising. "I will go at once. Did
she send — any — conveyance?"

"Catch her!" retorted the landlady. "Why,
she hain't had the town water let in yet — and she
wuth her fifteen thousand dollars; nor she won't
have no hired girl to do for her, not that none of

'em will stay along of her a week, and Dobson's boy's at the door, a drippin' and cussin' to get you, for he's nigh snowed under. She's a wuthless old heathen miser, the widder Peek."

"Then there is *every* reason why I should not neglect her," replied the clergyman, in his authoritative, clerical voice. "Pray call the lad in from the weather, and tell him I will accompany him at once."

He did look about his study sadly while he was making ready to leave it. The fire in the base-burner was quite warm, now, and his wet, much-darned stockings were beginning to dry. The room looked sheltered and pleasant; his books ran to the ceiling, though his floor was covered with straw matting, with odd pieces of woolen carpet for rugs; his carpet-covered lounge was wheeled out of the draft; his lamp with the green shade made a little circle of light and coziness; his Bible and prayer-book lay open within it, beside the pile of sermons. He had meant to devote the evening to the agreeable duty of selecting his discourse for Saint Agatha's. His mind and his heart were brimming over with the excitement of that great event. He would have liked to concentrate and consecrate his thoughts

upon it that evening. As he went, coughing, into
the cold entry, it occurred to him that the spot in
his lung was more painful than he had supposed;
but he pulled his old cap over his ears, and his thin
overcoat up to meet it, and tramped out cheerfully
into the storm.

"Well, well, my lad!" he said in his warm-
hearted way to Dobson's boy; "I'm sorry for you
that you have to be out a night like this."

The boy spoke of this afterwards, and remembered
it long — for a boy. But at the time he did but
stare. He stopped grumbling, however, and plunged
on into the drifts, ahead of the old rector, kicking
a path for him to right and left in the wet, packed
snow; for the widow Peek lived at least a mile away,
and the storm was now become a virulent thing.

What passed between the unloved, neglected,
dying parishoner and her pastor was not known to
any but themselves, nor is there witness now to tes-
tify thereof. Neither does it in any way concern
the record of this narrative, except as the least may
concern the largest circumstance in human story.
For, in view of what came to pass, it is impossible
not to put the old, judicial question : Did it pay?
Was it worth while? When the miser's soul went

out, at midnight, on the wings and the rage of that
blind, black storm, did it pass gently, a subdued,
forgiven spirit, humble to learn how to live again,
for Christ's sake and his who gave himself — as his
Master had before him — to comfort and to save?
Did it pay? *Do* such things pay? God knows.
But as long as men do not know, there will always
be found a few among them who will elect to dis-
regard the doubt, to wear the divinity of uncalcu-
lating sacrifice, and to pay its price.

For the soul of the widow Peek the price was
large, looked at in our mathematical way; for, when
the old clergyman, having shrived her soul and
closed her eyes, started to come home at one o'clock
of the morning, the storm had become a malignant
force. Already wet through and through his thin
coats and worn flannels, weak from the exposure, the
watching, and the scene of death, every breath a
sword athwart his inflamed lungs, with fire in his
brain, and ice at his heart, he staggered against the
blizzard.

Dobson's boy had long since sought the shelter
of his own home, and the old man was quite unat-
tended. True, the neighbor who watched with the
dead woman suggested that he remain till morning;

but the widow Peek's house was cold (she was always especially "near" about fuel), and he thought it more prudent to get back to his own stove and his bed.

Whether he lost his way; whether he crossed and recrossed it, wandering from it in the dark and drift; whether he fell and lay in the snow for a time, and rose again, and staggered on, and fell again, and so pushed on again, cannot be known. It is only known that at half-past two on Saturday morning his landlady put her wrinkled face out of the window, for the twentieth time, in search of him (for she had a thought for him in her own hard-featured way), and saw him fallen, and feebly trying to crawl on his hands and knees up the drifted steps.

She got him in to his warm study, past the chair where the flowered dressing-gown and old slippers awaited him, and as far as the carpet-covered lounge, Beyond this he could not be taken.

By morning the whole parish rang the door-bell; the hands and hearts and horses, the purses, the nurses, the doctors, the watchers, the tears, and the prayers of the village, were his — for he was dearly beloved and cherished in that parish. But he lay on his old lounge in his study among his books, and asked of them nothing at all. The kerosene lamp, behind its green shade, went out; and the Bible, with the pile of sermons on the table, looked large in the snow-light of a day when the storm ceases without sun. He did not talk; but his thoughts were yet alive. He remembered Saint Agatha's, and the sermon which he was to preach to-morrow. He knew that not one of his people (ignorant of such matters) would understand how to get word to the city vestry. He tried to give directions, but his voice refused his bidding. He knew that he would be supposed to have failed to meet his appointment, perhaps to have been thwarted — a rural clergyman, old and timorous, baffled in an important professional engagement — by a little snow. He was to have taken the evening train. He was to be the guest of the vestryman who wrote that pleasant letter. He was to preach in Saint Agatha's to-morrow. He was to —

Nay, — he was not, — nay. He was to do none of these things. A sick man, mortally a sick man, past power of speech, he lay upon his carpet lounge, shivering under the pile of thin blankets and cotton comforters that had been wrapped around him, and gently faced his fate. He could not preach at Saint Agatha's. And he could not explain to the vestry. Perhaps his heart-sickness about this matter subsided a little—one likes to think so—as his disease grew upon him; but there are men who will understand me when I say that this was the greatest disappointment of his humble, holy life.

As Saturday night drew on, and the stars came out, he was heard to make such efforts to speak articulately, that one of his weeping people (an affectionate woman of a brighter wit than the rest) made out, as she bent lovingly over him, to understand so much as this:

"Lord," he said, "into thy hands I commit my s-p—"

"He commits his spirit to the Lord!" sobbed the landlady.

But the listening parishioner raised her finger to her lips.

"Lord," he said again, and this time the dullest ear in the parish could have heard the words—"Lord," he prayed, "into thy hands I commit—my supply."

Sunday morning broke upon the city as cold and

clear as the sword of a rebuking angel. People on the way to the West End churches exchanged notes on the thermometer, and talked of the destitution of the poor. It was so cold that the ailing and the aged for the most part stayed at home. But the young, the *ennuyé*, the imitative, and the soul-sick, got themselves into their furs and carriages when the chimes rang, and the audiences were, on the whole, as comfortable and as devout as usual.

The vestryman sat nervously in his pew. He had not fully recovered from the fact that his supply had disappointed him. Having sent his coachman in vain to all the Saturday evening trains to meet his country parson, the vestryman had passed but an uneasy night.

"I had supposed the old man had principles about Sunday travel," he said to his wife, "but it seems he is coming in the morning, after all. He might at least have sent me word."

"Telegraphing in the country is — difficult, sometimes, I have heard," replied the lady, vaguely. She was a handsome, childless woman, with the haughty under lip of her class. Her husband spoke cheerily, but he was not at ease, and she did not know how to make him so.

The Sunday morning train came in from the
country station forty miles back, but the old clergyman was not among its passengers. Now thoroughly
alarmed, the vestryman had started for his hat and
coat, when his parlor-maid brought him a message.
It had been left at the door, she said, by a messenger who brooked neither delay nor question, but
ordered her to tell the master of the house that the
supply for Saint Agatha's was in the city, and would
meet the engagement at the proper time and place.
The old clergyman, the messenger added, had been
suddenly stricken with a dangerous illness, and
could not be expected; but his substitute would
fill the pulpit for the day. The vestryman was
requested to feel no concern in the matter. The
preacher preferred retirement until the hour of the
service, and would fulfil his duties at the church at
the appointed hour.

But when the vestryman, feeling flurried despite
himself, tapped at the door of the luxurious vestry-
room, gracefully refurnished that winter for the
rector with the sore throat who was in the south of
France, he found it locked; and to his unobtrusive
knock no answer came. At this uncomfortable moment the sexton tiptoed up to say that the supply

had requested not to be disturbed until the service should begin. The sexton supposed that the clergyman needed extra preparation; thought that perhaps the gentleman was from the country, and — ah — unused to the audience.

" What is his name? What does he look like?" asked the chairman, with knotted brows.

" I have not seen him sir," replied the sexton, with a puzzled expression.

" How did you receive the message?"

" By a messenger who would not be delayed or questioned."

Struck by the repetition of this phrase, the chairman asked again:

" But what did the messenger look like?" The sexton shook his head.

" I cannot tell you, sir. He was a mere messenger. I paid no attention to him."

" Very well," said the church officer, turning away discontentedly. " It must be all right. I have implicit confidence in the man whose chosen substitute this is."

With this he ceased to try to intrude himself upon the stranger, but went down to his pew, and sat beside his wife in uneasy silence.

The chimes sang and sank, and sang again:

Holy, holy, holy —

The air was so clear that the sound rang twice
the usual distance through the snowlit, sunlit air;
and the sick and the old at home listened to the
bells with a sudden stirring at their feeble hearts,
and wished again that they could have gone to
church. One bed-ridden woman, whose telephone
connected her with Saint Agatha's, held the receiver
to her sensitive ear, and smiled with the quick
gratitude for trifling pleasures of the long sick, as
she recognized the notes of the chime. With a leap
and a thrill as if they cast their metal souls out in
the act, the voices of the bells rose and swelled, and
ceased and slept, and where they paused the anthem
took the word up:

Holy, holy —

and carried it softly, just above the breath, with
the tone which is neither a sigh, nor a cry, nor a
whisper, but that harmony of all which makes of
music prayer.

He must have entered on the wave of this strain;
opinions differed afterwards as to this: some said one
thing, some another; but it was found that most of

the audience had not observed the entrance of the preacher at all. The choir ceased, and he was; and no more could be said. The church was well filled, though not over-crowded, and the decorous rustle of a fashionable audience in the interval preceding worship stirred through the house.

In the natural inattention of the moment, it was not remarkable that most of the people failed to notice the strange preacher until he was among them.

But to the church officer, whose mind was pre-occupied with the supply, there was something almost startling in the manner of his approach.

The vestryman's uneasy eyes were not conscious of having slipped their guard upon the chancel for a moment; he had but turned his head politely, though a bit impatiently, to reply to some trivial remark of his wife's, when, behold, the preacher stood before him.

Afterwards it was rumored that two or three persons in the audience had not been taken by surprise in this way, but had fully observed the manner of the stranger's entrance; yet these persons, when they were sought, were difficult to find. There was one shabby woman who sat in the gallery among the "poor" seats; she was clad in rusty mourning, and had a pale and patient face, quite familiar to the audience, for she was a faithful church-goer, and had attended Saint Agatha's for many years. It came to be said, through the sexton's gossip or otherwise, that this poor woman had seen the preacher's approach quite clearly, and had been much moved thereat; but when some effort was made to find her, and to question her on this point, unexpected obstacles arose, — she was an obscure person, serving in some menial capacity for floating employers; she was accustomed to slip in and out of the church hurriedly, both late and early, — and nothing of importance was added from this quarter to the general interest which attended the eccentricities of the supply.

The stranger was a man a trifle above the ordinary height, of majestic mien and carriage, and with the lofty head that indicates both fearlessness and purity of nature. As he glided to his place behind the lectern, a hush struck the frivolous audience, as if it had been smitten by an angel's wing: such power is there in noble novelty, and in the authority of a high heart.

When had the similar of this preacher led the

service in that venerable and fashionable house of worship? In what past years had his counterpart served them?

Whom did he resemble of the long line of eminent clerical teachers with whose qualities this elect people was familiar? What had been his history, his ecclesiastical position, his social connections? It was characteristic of the audience that this last question was first in the minds of a large proportion of the worshipers. Whence came he? His name? His titles? What was his professional reputation — his theology? What were his views on choir-boys, confessionals, and candles — on mission chapels and the pauperizing of the poor?

These inquiries swept through the inner consciousness of the audience in the first moment of his appearance. But in the second, neither these nor any other paltry queries fretted the smallest soul before him.

The stranger must have had an impressive countenance; yet afterwards it was found that no two descriptions of it agreed. Some said this thing, some said that. To this person he appeared a gentle, kindly man with a persuasive manner; to that, he looked majestic and commanding. There were some who spoke of an authoritative severity in the eye which he turned upon them; but these were not many. There were those who murmured that they had melted beneath the tenderness of his glance, as snow before the sun; and such were more. As to the features of his face, men differed, as spectators are apt to do about the lineaments of extraordinary countenances. What was the color of his eyes, the contour of his lips, the shape of his brow? Who could say? Conflicting testimony arrived at no verdict. In two respects alone opinions agreed about the face of this man: it commanded, and it shone; it had authority and light. The shrewdest heresy-hunter in the congregation would not have dared question this clergyman's theology, or the tendencies of his ritualistic views. The veriest pharisee in the audience quailed before the blinding brilliance of the preacher's face. It was a moral fire. It ate into the heart. Sin and shame shriveled before it.

One might say that all this was apparent in the preacher before he had spoken a word. When he had opened his lips these impressions were intensified. He began in the usual way to read the usual prayers, and to conduct the service as was expected of him. Nothing eccentric was observable in his treatment of the preliminaries of the occasion. The fashionable choir, accustomed to dictate the direction of the music, met with no interference from the clergyman. He announced the hymns and anthems that had been selected quite in the ordinary manner; and the critics of the great dailies took the usual notes of the musical programme. In fact, up to the time of the sermon, nothing out of the common course occurred.

But having said this, one must qualify. Was it nothing out of the common course that the congregation in Saint Agatha's should sit as the people sat that day, bond-slaves before the enunciation of the familiar phrases in the morning's confession?

"What a voice!" whispered the wife of the vestryman. But her husband answered her not a word. Pale, agitated, with strained eyes uplifted, and nervous hands knotted together, he leaned towards the stranger. At the first articulate sentence from the pulpit, he knew that the success of his supply was secured.

What a voice indeed! It melted through the great house like burning gold. The heart ran after it as fire runs through metal. Once or twice in a

generation one may hear the liturgy read like that
— perhaps. In a lifetime no longer to be counted
short, the vestryman had heard nothing that
resembled it.

"Thank God!" he murmured. He put his hat
before his face. He had not realized before what a
strain he had endured. Cold drops stood upon his
brow. He shook with relief. From that moment
he felt no more concern about the service than if he
had engaged one of the sons of God to "supply."

"Are you faint?" asked his wife in a tone of
annoyance. She offered him her smelling-salts.

Had there existed stenographic records of that
sermon, this narrative, necessarily so defective,
would have no occasion for its being. One of the
most interesting things about the whole matter is
that no such records can to-day be found. Reporters certainly were in the gallery. The journals had
sent their picked men as usual, and no more.
Where, then, were their columns of verbal record?
Why has so important a discourse gone afloat upon
vague, conflicting rumor? No person knows; the
reporters least of all. One, it is said, lost his
position for the default of that report; others

received the severest rebukes of their experience from their managing editors for the same cause. None had any satisfactory reason to give for his failure.

"I forgot," said he who lost his position for his boyish excuse. "All I can say, sir, is I forgot. The man swept me away. I forgot that such a paper as 'The Daily Gossip' existed. Other matters," he added with expensive candor, "seemed more important at the time."

.   .   .   .

"When the Son of Man cometh, shall he find faith on the earth?"

The stranger announced this not unusual text with the simple manner of a man who promised nothing eccentric in the sermon to come. Yet something in the familiar words arrested attention. The phrase, as it was spoken, seemed less a hackneyed biblical quotation than a pointed personal question to which each heart in the audience-room was compelled to respond.

The preacher began quietly. He reminded his hearers in a few words of the true nature of the Christian religion, whose interests he was there to represent. One felt that he spoke with tact, and

with the kind of dignity belonging to the enthusi-
ast of a great moral movement. It occurred to one,
perhaps for the first time, that it was quite manly
in a Christian preacher to plead his cause with as
much ardor as the reformer, the philanthropist, the
politician, or the devotee of a mystical and fashionable cult. One became really interested in the
character and aims of the Christian faith; it did
not fall below the dignity of a Browning society,
or a study in theosophy or hypnotism. The attention of the audience — from the start definitely
respectful — became reverent, and thus absorbed.

It was not until he had his hearers thoroughly in
his power that the preacher's manner underwent the
remarkable change of which Saint Agatha's talks in
whispers to this day. He spoke entirely without
manuscript or note, and he had not left the lectern.
Suddenly folding his hands upon the great Bible,
he paused, and, as if the audience had been one
man, he looked it in the eye.

Then, like the voice of the living God, his words
began to smite them. What was the chancel of
Saint Agatha's? The great white throne? And
who was he who dared to cry from it, like the
command of the Eternal? Sin! Sinners! Shame!

Guilt! Disgrace! Punishment! What words were these for the delicate ears of Saint Agatha's? What had these silken ladies and gilded men to do with such ugly phrases? Smiles stiffened upon refined, protesting faces. The haughty under lip of the vestryman's wife, and a hundred others like it, dropped. A moral dismay seized the exclusive people whom the preacher called to account like any vulgar audience. But the shabby woman in the "poor" seats humbly wept, and the young reporter who lost his position cast his eyes upon the ground, for the tears that sprang to them. From the delicate fingers of the vestryman's wife the smelling-salts fell upon the cushioned seat; she held her feathered fan against her face. Her husband did not even notice this. He sat with head bowed upon the rail before him, as a good man does when reconsecrating himself at the communion hour.

The choir rustled uneasily in their seats. The soprano covered her eyes with her well-gloved hand, and thought of the follies and regrets (she called them by these names) that beset the musical temperament. But the tenor turned his face away, and thought about his wife. Down the avenue, in the room of the "shut-in" woman, where the tele-

phone carried the preacher's voice, a pathetic cry
was heard :

"Forgive! Forgive! Oh, if suffering had but
made me better!"

But now the preacher's manner of address had
changed again. Always remembering that it is now
impossible to quote his language with any accuracy,
we may venture to say that it ran in some such way
as this :

The Son of God, being of the Father, performed
his Father's business. What do ye who bear his
name? What holy errands are ye about? What
miracles of consecration have ye wrought? What
marvels of the soul's life have ye achieved upon the
earth since he left it to your trust?

He came to the sinful and the unhappy; the
despised and rejected were his friends; to the poor
he preached the Gospel; the sick, and overlooked,
and cast-out, the unloved and forgotten, the un-
fashionable and unpopular, he selected. These to
his church on earth he left in charge. These he
cherished. For such he had lived. For them he
had suffered. For them he died. People of Saint
Agatha's, where *are* they? What have ye done to
his beloved? Thou ancient church, honored and

privileged and blessed among men, where are those little ones whom thy Master chose? Up and down these godly aisles a man might look, he said, and see them not. Prosperity and complacency he saw before him; poverty and humility he did not see. In the day when habit cannot reply for duty, what account will ye give of your betrayed trust? Will ye say: "Lord, we had a mission chapel. The curate is responsible for the lower classes. And, Lord, we take up the usual collections; Saint Agatha's has always been called a generous church"?

In the startled hush that met these preposterous words the preacher drew himself to his full height, and raised his hand. He had worn the white gown throughout the day's services, and the garment folded itself about his figure majestically. In the name of Christ, then, he commanded them: Where were those whom their Lord did love? Go, seek them. Go, find the saddest, sickest souls in all the town. Hasten, for the time is short. Search, for the message is of God. Church of Christ, produce his people to me, for I speak no more words before their substitutes!

Thus and there, abruptly, the preacher cast his audience from him, and disappeared from the chancel. The service broke in consternation. The celebrated choir was not called upon to close the morning's worship. The soprano and the tenor exchanged glances of neglected dismay. The prayer-book remained unopened on the sacred desk. The desk itself was empty. The audience was, in fact, authoritatively dismissed — dismissed without a benediction, like some obscure or erring thing that did not deserve it.

The people stared in one another's faces for an astounded moment, and then, without words, with hanging heads, they moved to the open air and melted out of the church.

The sexton rushed up to the vestryman, pale with fear.

"Sir," he whispered, "he is not in the vestry-room. He has taken himself away — God knows whither. What are we to do?"

"Trust him," replied the church officer, with a face of peace, "and God who sent him. Who he may be, I know no more than you; but that he is a man of God I know. He is about his Father's business. Do not meddle with it."

"Lord forbid!" cried the sexton. "I'd sooner meddle with something I can understand."

Upon the afternoon of that long-remembered Sunday there was seen in Saint Agatha's the strangest sight that those ancient walls had witnessed since the corner-stone was laid with a silver trowel in the name of the Father and of the Son and of the Holy Ghost "whom we, this people, worship."

Before the chimes rang for the vesper service, the house was filled. Before the bronze lips of the bells were mute, the pews were packed. Before the stranger reappeared, the nave and the transept overflowed. The startled sexton was a leaf before the wind of the surging crowd. He could not even enforce the fire-laws, and the very aisles were jammed. Who carried the story? How do such wraiths of rumors fly?

Every member of that church not absent from town or known to be ill in his bed sought his pew that afternoon. Many indeed left their sick-rooms to be present at that long-remembered service. But no man or woman of these came alone. Each brought a chosen companion; many, two or three; some came accompanied by half a dozen worshipers: and upon these invited guests Saint Agatha's looked with an astonishment that seemed to be half shame;

for up those velvet aisles there moved an array of human faces at which the very angels and virtues in the painted windows seemed to turn their heads and stare.

Such wretchedness, such pallor, hunger, cold, envy, sickness, sin, and shame were as unknown to those dedicated and decorated walls as the inmates of hell.   Rags and disease, uncleanliness and woe and want, trod the house of God as if they had the right there.   Every pew in the church was thrown open.   Tattered blanket shawls jostled velvet cloaks, and worn little tan-colored reefers, half concealing the shivering cotton blouses of last summer, rubbed against sealskin furs that swept from throat to foot. Wretched men, called in by the throb of repentance that follows a debauch, lifted their haggard eyes to the chancel from the pews of the wardens, and women of the town sat gently beside the " first ladies " of the parish and of the city.   There were a few ragged children in the audience, wan and shrewd, sitting drearily beside mothers to whom they did not cling.   The pew of our friend, the vestryman, was filled to overflowing.   The wife with the under lip sat beside him, and did not protest.   She had herself gone with him to the hospital to select their guests. For their pew was filled with the crippled and other sick who could neither walk nor afford to ride, and whom their own carriage had brought to Saint Agatha's. One of these, a woman, came on crutches, and the lady helped her, not knowing in the least how to do it; and a man who had not used his feet for six years was lifted in by the pew-owner and his coachman and butler, and carried the length of the broad aisle.

The church, as we say, was packed long before the preacher appeared. He came punctually to his appointment, like any ordinary man. It was mid-afternoon, and the sun was declining when he glided across the chancel. Already shadows were lying heavily in the corners of the church and under the galleries on the darker side. A few lights were glimmering about the chancel, but these served only to illuminate the stranger's form and face; they did not lighten the mass of hushed and appealing humanity before him.

The choir, with bowed heads, just above the breath, began to chant:

> Who shall lay anything to the charge
> Of God's Elect ?
> It is God that justifieth,
> It is Christ that died.

While they sang the preacher stood quite still and looked at the people, that strange and motley mass, the rich and the poor, the sick and the well, the disgraced and the reputable, the pampered and the starving, the shameful and the clean of life, the happy and the wretched together. When the singing ceased, he spoke as if he talked right on; he read no prayers; he turned to no ritual; he did not even use the great Bible of Saint Agatha's — but only spoke in a quiet way, like a man who continues a thought begun:

"For the Lord," he said, "is the maker of you all."

There was no sermon in Saint Agatha's that afternoon. Ecclesiastically speaking, there was no service. But the preacher spoke to the people; and their hearts hung upon his words. But what those words were no man may tell us at this day.

It has been whispered, indeed, that what he said took different meanings to the members of that strange audience. Each heart received its own message. Wide as the earth were the gulfs between those hearers. But the preacher's message bridged them all. From his quivering lip and melting voice each soul drank the water of life. Afterwards each kept its own secret, and told not of that thirst, or of its assuaging.

"He speaks to me," sighed the patrician, with bowed head. "How happens this, for I thought no man did know that inner history? I have never told" —

"To me! To me!" sobbed the pauper and the castaway — "the preacher speaks to me. My misery, my shame — the whole world knows, but no man ever understood before."

The afternoon waned. The shadows deepened under the galleries. The great house clung like one child to the voice of the preacher. It was as still as the courts of Heaven when a soul is pardoned. The stranger spoke in a low but penetrating voice. Not a word was lost by the remotest. He spoke of the love of God the Father, and of the life of Christ the Son. He spoke of sin and of forgiveness, of sorrow, of shame, and of peace. He spoke of sacrifice, of patience, of purity, and of hope, and of the eternal life.

Not once did he allude to the petty differences among the people who sat bowed and breathless before him. Such paltry things as riches or poverty, or position, or obscurity, he did not recognize.

He spoke to men and women, the children of God.
He spoke to sinners and to sufferers, and to patient
saints; he said nothing about "classes;" he talked
of human beings; he rebuked them for their sins;
he comforted them for their miseries; he smote their
hearts; he shook their souls; he passed over their
lives as conflagration passes, burning to ashes, puri-
fying to new growth.

As he spoke, the manner of his countenance
changed before them, like that of any great and holy
man who is charged with the burden of souls, and
who persuadeth them. A fine, inner light glowed
through his features, as a sacred lamp glows through
alabaster or some exquisite shell. His plaintive lip
trembled. His deep eyes burned and retreated, as
if they veiled themselves. An expression dazzling
to behold settled upon his face. His white garment
gathered light, and shone. Suddenly pausing, he
stretched forth his hands. What delicate arrange-
ment of the chancel lamps illuminated them? It was
noticed by many, and spoken of afterwards below
the breath. For, as he raised them in benediction
upon the people, there scintillated from the palms a
light. Some said that it was reflected from the
radiance of the man's face. Some said that it had

" The face of the stranger swam before her "

another cause. Only this is sure: when he did uplift his hands to bless them, all the people fell upon their knees before him.

It was now almost dark in the church, and no man could see his neighbor's face. The choir, on their knees, began to sing, "Holy, holy, holy"— When their voices fell, the preacher's rose:

" And now may the grace of God the Father, and the love of Jesus Christ his Son, your Lord, and the peace of the Holy Spirit, be upon you; for there is Life Eternal; and God is the Light thereof; whose children ye are forever. Amen, and Amen."

His voice ceased. The hush that followed it was broken only by sobs.

The electric lights sprang out all over the church. In the sudden brilliance the kneeling people lifted their wet faces to the stranger's, thinking to catch a last sight of him for life-long treasure.

But the chancel was empty. As silently, as strangely, as he had come, the preacher had gone. It was the fashion of the man. Such was his will. He was never seen at Saint Agatha's again; nor, though his name and fame were widely sought, were they ever learned by any.

The great, strange crowd of worshipers melted